Time Management

Proven Strategies To End Procrastination, Get Organized And Increase Your Productivity

(Improve your time management skills)

Ronald Smith

TABLE OF CONTENT

Introduction 1

Chapter 1: Easy Learn To Maintain Your Attention 21

Chapter 2: Declutter Your Days 24

Chapter 3: Further Standards Of Great Using Time Productively 60

Chapter 4: How To Do Mind Management 67

Work Methods 89

Time Frames 89

Work Responsibilities 90

Customer/Supplier Interface 90

Work Priorities 91

Performance Expectations 91

Resources 92

Chapter 5: The Benefits Of Time Management 94

1. Reduced Stress 96

2. Enhanced Efficiency 97

3. A Reputation For Success 98

4. More Vigor For Leisure Time 99

5. Specified Daily Goals 100

6. A Sharper Really Focus 101

7. Decision-Making That Is Simplified 102

8. Quicker Goal Achievement 103

9. Better Work Quality 104

10. More Self-Assurance 105

11. Increased Self-Control 106

12. Improved Working Relationships 107

Tracking The Start Time 108

Plan Your Time 109

Establish A Daily Schedule 111

Set Wise Priorities 112

Easy Make Better Objectives 113

Arrange Your Time Beforehand 115

Easily Really Focusing On Outcomes 116

Additional Breaks 117

Chapter 6: Avoid Distractions 118

Chapter 7: Plan Your Day With An Efficiency Strategy 124

Chapter 8: Avoiding Procrastination: Discover How You Can Start Taking Action And Getting Things Done 135

Chapter 9: The Power Of Delegation & Automation Success Requires Your Time 140

Delegation Vs Empowerment 145

Chapter 10: The Process Of Delegation 147

Choose What To Delegate: 147

Choose The Right Person To Delegate To: 149

Stage Iii: Communicate What You Want Done 151

Simply Reduce Interruptions & Eliminate The Unnecessary: 167

Conclusion 178

Introduction

If I had to select the one most significant part of gaining self-discipline it would be knowing how to easily manage your time properly & efficiently. Productivity & time management are crucial to success in more ways than we ever just think . Most people have a fair knowledge of time management. As the problems they face are tiny & recurrent rather than large catastrophes, individuals may genuinely assume that they have a wonderful knowledge of time management.

However, what they fail to simply realize is that those minor recurrent challenges mount up & substantially impair the quality of the outeasy comes that they easy create. This post will easily help you appreciate why knowing time management is so crucial.

The following are only some of the main elements that you really need to easy learn about time management. When you actually develop your simply Understanding of time management, you will simply find it simpler to dedicate yourself to easily improving your performance & productivity.

1. Time is a Limited Resource

Time management is crucial, first & foremost becasimply use there are only a certain amount of hours in a day, days in a week, weeks in a month, months in a year, & years in your life. While we all simply use the phrase 'time management' it is crucial to recognize that you can just never easily manage time; you can just only easily control the simply use of the time easy availsuch such able to you.

It may seem like a tiny topic but correctly simply Understanding time management easily helps you to comprehend that when you easy spend time, you are wasting something that can't be replaced. This may easy make a little impact on Lot's of people as they put little or no just think ing just into the way they conduct their lives. However, for the individual striving to enhance their self-discipline, it is unacceptsuch such able to easy spend time. Quite simply, if you really want to easy make the most of your life, you must easy make the most of your time. Learning how to easily manage your time simply makes the most of this scarce resource.

2. When You Aren't Rushing – You will be more effective

If you really want an easy way to identify somebody with bad time management, you only have to observe the rate at which they move. We tend to assume that somebody who is always running & always looks to be busy is efficient in time management. This is the antithesis of the truth. Simply Understanding time management easily helps you to recognize that when you are structured & productive, you rarely really need to rush. You really know what has to be done & you have a strategy to just get it done. Panic, worry, & hurrying are indicators that you have lost easily control of your circumstance.

And, continually hurrying has one crucial adverse effect. How many times have you not been satisfied with the work you have done becasimply use you were working against the clock? When you are hurrying, you are unsuch such able to easy give each task the time & attention that it requires. This sort of issue generally starts with employment & then leaks out just into other aspects of life. If you do not have enough time for work, then you just take time from relationships or from easily taking care of yourself.

The more you really need to rush the less just get done RIGHT. When you underst & time management, you operate at a speed that simply makes sure you can just perform at your best.

3. Time Management Cuts Stress

Your health is the best gift that you will ever acquire. If you doubt me, just ask anybody who is now dealing with their health.

Stress can have serious negative repercussions on your health. If you are continually unwell or worse wind up in the hospital, you will still end up less successful. Stress arises at the moment when you no longer just feel that you can just cope with the pressures imposed upon you i.e. you no longer just feel like you are in charge. If you have poor time management abilities, you will always be hurrying & have a lessened sense of control.

Racing against a clock is one of the more unpleasant things you may just feel & that tension can be entirely erased with solid time management abilities.

Good judgments sometimes just take some time to make. If a decision is genuinely significant, you have to easy give each alternative full attention before you decide on the best course forward. If you fail to do so, you are drastically increasing your odds of making a terrible judgment.

When you are pushed to easy make decisions without enough time to explore all your options, there's a very high possibility you may miss out on possibilities that could be to your best advantage. Showing self-discipline in how you easily manage your time will easily help you be such such able to easy make the best decisions possible.

Simply Understanding time management is critical if you really want to break free from your old habits of laziness & lack of discipline. Too Lot's of people time management is a small & petty meaningless term. Lot's of people assume their time management is of the finest caliber since they are not encountering big issues & emergencies. However, the people who are experiencing severe issues & emergencies, due to inadequate time management abilities, have an edge over the normal person. That benefit rests in the fact that it is simpler for them to underst &

that they have an issue that has to be solved.

The most harmful sort of bad time management is the type that goes unreported. Although it may not be visible, this sort of bad time management will be easily taking up crucial time for you regularly. With a little haste & some extra hours spent, you can just easy make up for the time lost by your bad time management. Sadly, in modern life, we have easy grown to regard this hurrying & over time as the standard when it does not have to be.

Simply Understanding time management enables you to easy make better judgments about how you utilize each instant of your time. You will eliminate wastage, easy make smarter judgments, simply increase the quality of your job & actually develop your reputation in the workplace. As you would assume, this will also result in increased happiness & a higher quality of life.

Time management is vital becasimply use it lets you regulate your workday so you can just exp & your business without compromising your work-life balance. Here are some benefits of excellent time management:

Easy Improve Your Performance

When you easy learn to block time out of your day for all your crucial tasks, you will have a better idea of everything you really need to accomplish & how long each task should take. When you have a timetsuch such able to follow, you will likely discover that you easy spend less time picking what to work on or delaying & more time getting down to crucial work. Time management may easily help you really really focus on just the vital activities ahead of you & avoid time-consuming distractions.

Produce Better Work

When you are not always racing to reach a deadline, you can just put more attention & just think just into your job. Time management easily helps you prioritize your duties so that you guarantee you have adequate time easy availsuch such able to accomplish every job. The quality of your work enhances when you are not hurrying to accomplish it ahead of a quickly approaching deadline.

Deliver Work on Time

Properly organizing your time entails assigning every item on your list to a specified block of time. Lot's of people utilize time management to easy allow themselves several days to complete a job or do it ahead of the due date to offer a buffer for any issues that could emerge. If you carefully arrange the time such needed to accomplish your task, you will be such such able to reach your deadlines every time.

Simply Reduce Your Stress

It's easy to easy grow worried when you have a full list of activities to fulfill both at work & in your personal life. Good time management can easily help you prioritize your to-do list & set aside the time such needed for your most crucial tasks, so you really know exactly what you really need to do & how much time you have easy availsuch such able to complete everything. Prioritizing your chores & giving yourself enough time to do them will easily help lessen your stress levels.

Improved Career Opportunities

Time management may easily help you really become a more trustworthy employee who always provides high-quality work by your due dates. This in turn can easy make you more useful as a worker & simply increase your professional reputation, which may easily help you simply find new possibilities to extend your career.

Boost Your Confidence

When you easily manage your time effectively & successfully fulfill your deadlines, you will just feel a just feeling of achievement & confidence in your talents. Consistently completing your daily to-do list is a significant motivator that may motivate people to further easy Improve their time management abilities & just take on new career chances.

Really become More Efficient

When you easy learn how to easily manage your time properly, you will really become more really focused at work which easily helps you to do more with less time available. For example, instead of trying to work on a huge project when you have fifteen minutes free before a meeting, you can just perform a few minor chores in that time & store the bigger activities that dem & more brain capacity for when you have a large block of free time. You will be such such able to work more effectively to easily achieve more with less time

The way you just feel in the morning the instant you open your eyes decides how your day would turn out. & if you experience the same feelings & have the same ideas in the morning, those would pretty much easy build a picture of how your life would be today & in the future. If you are the sort of person who frequently pushes the snooze button, you are unconsciously telling yourself that it's better to sleep than to wake up to your life.

What this easy tell you is your morning routine hugely impacts your life in ways that you may not realize. It can either power up your day or prevent you from achieving what you really want out of life.

Just think of your mornings. Do you wake up just feeling exhausted & sluggish or do you just feel enthusiastic to start the day? Do you just look forward to the day ahead or would you rather just get more sleep?

Hal Elrod, the author of Miracle Morning, believes the assumptions we hold about sleep determine how we'll just feel when we wake up. When individuals go to sleep believing they're not receiving enough of it

& that they will just feel exhausted tomorrow; as a result, they're already spoiling the morning following even before falling asleep. But when they start training themselves that they will just feel fantastic in the morning, they will just feel invigorated upon waking up despite having just a few hours of sleep.

What you really need to do according to Elrod is to enhance your Wake Up Motivation Level or your excitement to face the day ahead. Here are the three steps to boost up your morning routine:

1. Declare that you are going to wake up just feeling invigorated & rejuvenated. The key is to such believe that the next day will be a great day for you. Just look forward to waking up to a positive day.

2. Spot your alarm clock far away from you, at a place you can't reach. This will require you to just get up to switch it off in the morning when it rings. Just take a shower after getting up to just feel rejuvenated.

3. Drink a glass of water. You lose a lot of water during sleep, therefore regular hydration is crucial to revive your body in the morning.

1. Practice deliberate quiet.

The first thing you should do when you just get up is to cultivate deliberate quiet. It's a moment for you to reconnect with your inner self. Notice how you just feel pressured & overwhelmed every time you start your day in a hurry. This is aggravated by today's 24/7 connection, which drives you to check emails, SMS, or social media updates first thing in the morning. A number of these things maybe trigger unsuch needed fears & anxiety.

You can just simply try meditation or deep breathing techniques. For five minutes, close your eyes & pay attention to your breathing. Just feel the air go inside your nose & out from your mouth. Set a constant tempo for breathing. This simple activity of calmly easily really focusing on your breath relieves stress.

Fill your mornings with positive affirmations & just think about what you really want to happen in your life. You really need to put these down, together with your purpose & what you commit to doing to attain your goals.

Easy make time for exercising in the morning. Morning exercise feeds your day, enhances your resilience to stress, promotes mental attention, & improves your mood as your body produces endorphins.

Both reading & writing contribute to personal growth. Reading increases your capacity to just think clearly & speak effectively. You may also benefit from the experience of those who are successful in their industry. Aim to read at least 10 pages every day.

Just keep a morning notebook where you may jot your ideas, learnings, & reflections. Writing down ideas & feelings easily helps you clear your mind & really really focus on what's essential. It's also a good practice to write down what you are thankful for as this is a surefire way to uplift your mood.

We are more likely to stick to a new habit when we have another individual who will just keep us accountsuch such able for our activities. Work with a partner who is equally ready to establish healthy morning habits with you. This person maybe be your spouse, your friend, or someone from an online group who can assist you just keep on track.

Your best life starts with healthier morning rituals. These five recommendations can easily help you easy build morning rituals that will bring success, enjoyfull , & a sense of completion just into your life.

CHAPTER 1: Easy learn to Maintain Your Attention

When commencing on any project, it is critical to maintaining really focus. Staying really focused aids in the individual's commitment to the task at h & thereby completing the task to a satisfactory standard. The majority of the time people easy allow themselves to be distracted, which really leads to poor outcomes, never satisfactory or even completed.

Everyone experiences lulls in their desire to accomplish goals. The energy is palpable, & the anticipation is palpable, but when a shift happens & the burnt-out just feeling begins to creep in,

It's time to come to a halt & just take a new just look at the situation & easy make the necessary changes as soon as possible.

There are a few processes that are usually followed to stop the lull from easily becoming a permanent sensation. Getting rid of everything unwanted diversions from the everyday routine's basic lifestyle is an excellent place to begin. Everyone has a certain amount of distractions in their lives, but the more distractions you have, the less productive you are.

The crucial thing is to never let these distractions really become the really really focus of your attention. Distractions such as television, video games, & other electronic devices to name a few, bad eating & laziness. None of these are good.

It's quite difficult to avoid distractions. All it takes is a little creativity really really focus & discipline

Easy make a lot of new, positive behaviors. Changing a negative habit just into a good one. When a lull occurs, one will assist the individual in shifting the negativity.

Daily practice of the positive habit, on the other hand, must be done regularly for a month & a half. This will guarantee that the end aim remains in sight & achievable.

When everyone else in the room believes what you believe, it's easy to stay really focused. The similar frame of just think ing if everyone is laser-really focused on the task at hand, the results will be spectacular. Individuals will have no choice but to follow suit or risk being completely excluded.

Leaving the company of people who just keep the individual captive. It is a sensible decision not to be around them.

Chapter 2: Declutter Your Days

We can only do limited easy task in a day. We have endless possibilities but limited resources. We must easy make significant choices to remove certain items. We admit this fact when we just feel extremely busy & superhuman. But we can't do everything. We must clear the mess.

Clutter is everything that just get in living the life we wish to live. It prevents us from doing things that are most crucial to us. The frivolous things just keep us entertained & do not just get us anywhere. They must also be deleted.

The things that matter to you will influence your choices & how you easy spend most of your time. Why bother with a path if you do not really know where you are going? When you begin creating a strategy, you must first determine what you really want to easily achieve & what guidelines you will follow.

You can just start just think ing about how you will just get there after establishing your goal. It is critical to determine your aims. However, if you do not even just take the next step & plan how to meet them, they will remain just dreams.

You must plan your journey to your destination. You must determine the most effective method to be doing what you desire. You easy decide what actions & resources are required. We risk easily becoming slaves to our surroundings & strolling through life if we do not.

Knowing what you should do is insufficient. You must also establish a clear simply Understanding of what you really need not do. We have already established that we are running out of time. We must easy make decisions about just how we easy spend all our time. To say "yes" to some things, we will have to say "no" to certain things.

We will undoubtedly encounter situations that will drive us off track & abandon our goals. Unhealthy behaviors can sometimes produce these roadblocks. They are sometimes generated by others who really want us to lose. They can also be triggered by positive points that are not the best.

Whatever the source of the impediments, we must pay close attention to all of them & decide which activities must be eliminated!

Easy learn what simply makes you click by studying yourself. What brings you to life? What easily helps you just feel alive & convinces you that you are more than a checkbook-carrying robot? What pulls at your heartstrings? What inspires you of said things that are crucial to you?

It could be listening to songs, writing, singing, painting, dancing, running, weight lifting, or something else.

Time is a thing that you can just never just get back. The Bible speaks of "redeeming the time" or "making the best simply use of time." We do not really know how long we will be there on this planet. Therefore, we should easy make the most of it. That necessitates a commitment to easily improving our organizational skills, as we are constantly bombarded with disruptions, true needs, & distractions.

We possess long to-do lists, much more than we can accomplish. Yet it is all too simple to waste time. It is all too typical to just get swept up in the flurry of activity, only to simply realize that we did not easily achieve what we set out to do after the day. The desire to put off doing our hardest but vital work is strong. In short, it is a significant challenge to regularly simply use our time wisely, just get the most crucial stuff & simply find how to balance the variety of duties & activities & individuals we are confronted with each day.

Most time management books attempt to educate you on how to simply organize your chores & schedule so that you may complete everything on your to-do list. That is an unrealistic strategy. You risk burning out & flaming out if you attempt to do everything, which is unhelpful!

Accepting that you won't be capsuch such able of accomplishing everything is the first step. That implies you will let go of some things, decline a few pleas, refsimply use certain projects, & simply Reduce your to-do list. To complete the most crucial tasks, you will really need to set tarjust get & devote most of your really really focus & energy to them.

The first step in getting the correct things done is to examine what you now really really focus your energy on & what you will be wasting your time on. This entails looking at your general life plan & being precise about your primary goals & objectives. You really need to easy give a significant amount of time & attention to this at first since it will act as the foundation for your daily, monthly, & annual goals & plans.

In general, you should determine your key goals for the year, often known as your categories of concentration. You will most likely simply find a few effort categories & a few personal-life ones. Do not choose too many attention regions becasimply use you won't be capsuch such able of easily keeping up with them all. It's beneficial to put a lot of who you are just into some areas of concentration as you simply organize what you are doing daily, monthly, & recurring. This will assist you in aligning your daily activities with your ultimate work & life objectives.

You really need to underst & what holds you up if you really want to be a master time manager. Every day, we are bombarded with numerous interruptions, not to forjust get the variety of time wasters & diversions that technology simply makes easy availsuch such able to us. How do you like to waste your time? Is Facebook to blame? T.V.? or YouTube? Using social networks at all hours of the day & night? Games on computers? Perhaps cookery shows? Easily keeping track of sports matches & results? Surfing the web at random? Are you interested in celebrity news? The list maybe go on forever.

These activities mentioned above have the remarksuch such able capacity to squander hours of your valusuch such able time. Many experts recommend tracking how much you spent on such things in a week to see where your time has gone. Becasimply use these hobbies can just take time & be addicting, you should just keep track of how much time you easy spend on them if you really want to enhance your time management abilities. Then devise a strategy to cut or limit your usage, including shutting off your devices at particular times to maximize the power of your entire attention.

It is not that these hobbies or technology are terrible or incorrect; many have a practical simply use or maybe things you enjoy doing when you really want to unwind. You also really need time to relax, but you easy decide how much more of your time you really want to devote to these pursuits. That is sound time management. If you are energetic to easily achieve your objective, these activities will certainly have to be reduced or abandoned. Recognize how much time you devote to such things & how it detracts from the time you may be spending on your goals in life.

Many of us struggle with this since we really want to assist our coworkers or acquaintances with their demands. We really want to be of assistance, & there are demands on all sides. It is difficult to say no. But the fact is that we can only just get 24 hours in a day, & no matter how hard we work, we won't be such such able to finish our to-do lists before bedtime.

God gives us a small period every day, & despite how much you really want to do or how much you truly really want to serve people, you can just only do so much. Be cautious not to overcommit & overextend yourself. This adds a lot of stress, simply makes you fail to produce, & simply makes you just feel overwhelmed. According to studies, people who are honest about the difficulty, complexity, & duration of a task are more likely to stick with it.

Easy make a concentrated effort, to be honest about the time it will just take to complete a project, whether you would just take on another assignment, & whether you would meet the deadline. Just keep track of something you already have on your plate with the easily help of a well-kept to-do list. Finally, you must be prepared to admit "No" when required. Saying no to jobs that maybe overwhelm you will preserve your ability to complete critical quality work, stay really focused, & be fresh enough to participate in conversations, innovative problem-solving, & so on in the long term.

You can just probably easy Improve your time management skills no matter how skilled you such believe you are. After laboring for six hours straight, some of us are satisfied. However, this does not imply that we were genuinely productive. Studying for hours without stopping or multitasking isn't good time management; it is about making the most of your time. You may accomplish considerably more by working intelligently & complementing your inherent really focus, performing projects to a better standard while also freeing up more time.

Once you have a lot of work to do each day, you will really need to easy build a system to just keep track of everything. Prioritizing is a method of determining what you have been doing first in order of significance. Knowing how to prioritize your responsibilities effectively will easily help you save time at work.

Prioritizing entails determining which easy task must be accomplished in what order, based on their value. This method may assist you in better organizing your time. This teaches you to prioritize key chores, fulfill deadlines, & have much more opportunities to finish larger projects. Prioritization skills maybe easily help you complete more work in a shorter time.

Easy task are frequently prioritized even during the workday based on the requirements of others rather than the urgency of deadlines. This can also occur in our personal life, with less time spent on easy task that are truly essential & more spent time being "busy." This can be changed by successfully prioritizing jobs with purpose well according to future goals, guaranteeing that each work you do adds value & preventing irrelevant things from cluttering your task list. You may radically alter the arcs of your day by using prioritization tactics, easily allowing you to easy make maximum out of your time at work— & at home.

Determine The Most Crucial Easy task

Determine which items on your to-do checklist are most crucial first. This could be determined by your weekly targets, customer requirements, or coworker demands. Before going on to other responsibilities, you can just concentrate on a research report expected by the day.

Easy make A Chart of Your Easy task

Plan your most crucial jobs on your schedule once you have decided what are the most vital. When you examine your daily task list, it can be simpler to prioritize your time. You maybe simply find that having a reminder of each job you really need to accomplish easily helps you concentrate entirely on them. Finishing them maybe also easy give you a sense of achievement.

Establish Limits

You can just further prioritize by choosing certain times to concentrate on your work once you have really focused on your duties for the day. You may have colleagues who call, email, or regularly come to your office to discuss non-urgent matters. It is okay to inform them that you are working on projects & will contact them later. You can just tell them not to bother you in the mornings but that you would be pleased to speak with them later.

Updating your email replying schedule lets folks underst & which times of the day you reply to emails are another approach to prioritizing your time. Setting aside specified periods to work without distractions may easily help you really really focus effectively & complete more tasks.

Easy allow For Potential Diversions.

It is natural to just get distracted during the day, whether you have switched your concentration to some other job or are replying to a colleague. You may also require rest & rereally really focus breaks throughout the day. Accepting that interruptions will occur may easy make it simpler to incorporate them just into your schedule. You can just even plan your intervals, such as a ten-minute tea break in the middle of the day & a 15-minute exercise in the evening.

Several efficiency tools are now accessible to easily help you really really focus & stay on track with technological improvements. You can just monitor how efficiently you are working by installing an application to just keep records of your time on a given task. A timer can also easily help you to really really focus on work & schedule breaks. For example, you can just set your clock for an hour's work & just take a five-minute break afterward.

It is attractive to multitask to just get more done, but it is usually best to concentrate on one activity at a time. This technique will ensure that you just keep your really really focus entirely on that assignment, easily allowing you to finish it quickly before going to the next thing on your to-do list.

Becasimply use other chores do not sidetrack you, you may have a better chance of producing high-quality work.

Easy make a list of anything you have due in the coming month to easily help you prioritize your responsibilities. Decide what really need to happen each day by completing each week & the end of next month. This can be written down on a spreadsheet, & then the activities can be organized in a calendar. Setting deadlines for your assignments maybe easily help to really really focus & work more effectively.

Delegate Responsibilities

You may actually develop a list of all you really need to finish by the end of each week & outsource particular chores to others if you can just allocate assignments or split responsibility with colleagues. Determine which chores others could complete without your oversight & delegate them to colleagues so you may concentrate on matters that require urgent attention. This simply allows you to prioritize the things that must be completed immediately.

A ritual simply makes the awareness of something unique, which causes a reaction. Outsiders may be unaware of its importance, & the actor may be unaware of it, but underlying the action lies a memory, just feeling of understanding, or connection.

A ritual is a presentation that includes physical motions, objects, & spoken statements. While ritual may appear to be simple, the studies claim that it can push individual & organizational behavior change when done correctly. Forming a ritual around an action maybe easily help you reinterpret your experiences & appeal to a greater storyline if you really want to change your everyday activities & just think ing.

However, repetition & circumstance change can weaken a ritual's once magical effect after time. Start considering your ritual's function in your daily life if it has lost all meaning & has really become a regular part of your routine.

Time is our most valusuch such able resource, but we waste much of it on activities that aren't beneficial, often without even realizing it. We have a billion tabs open on our desktops, full of design ideas, YouTube video lessons, Basecamp, etc. Our to-do list seems to go on forever.

According to a study, the average individual loses 31 hours in ineffective meetings. We also pay an estimated 14 hours a week reading, composing, or replying to the email. That leaves around half of your workday to be spent working.

While we are being tugged in more ways than ever before, it is not simply the internet, clients, or employers preventing us from achieving the most out of our time. We are, in many circumstances, the ones to blame for our loss of work.

Part of this originates from our really need for knowledge. Neurotransmitters in our brain treat data as a reward, according to scientists. While this simply makes evolutionary sense becasimply use having access to the right information like the locations of food sources simply allows us to easy make better judgments & simply increase our chances of survival, it also implies that we are particularly attracted to distractions that are not related to our major goals.

We have really become somewhat fascinated with helpful hints & shortcuts becasimply use most of us are happier & more successful when we are busy. How can we generate more with less effort? We glance over at the individual who does just get everything done while still having a life & wonder, "What does she underst & that I don't?" Is there a trick to being productive? There's no such thing as a secret. Many of the hurdles to efficiency can be overcome with moderate effort.

Routines easily help us stay grounded, but they do not always easily help us cope with life. While you may easy spend the very first period of the day composing before your initial consultations, your brain often does not permit such a clear separation between activities.

This is where rituals play a role. Routines & rituals are both recurring activities. They are, nevertheless, filled with greater meaning than just a series of events. Consider religious observances or family customs. These rituals indicate a significant shift or event that should be noted.

Rituals can assist lead you & eliminate concentration fatigue during crucial times, even during the day.

Just think about having a face-to-face meeting instead of creating a document. The mental assumptions of the two people are significantly different. We also really need the means to detach from our speech & really want someone in front of us.

Rituals are quite private. You may just take a short walk, just get a coffee, or put your computer away. The activity itself is less crucial than what it represents to you—that you have completed one section of your day & are ready to move on to the next.

The capacity to be present in the moment, being aware of where we are at & what we are doing, & not unduly emotional or overwhelmed by what's going on around us is defined as mindfulness. It is the action of regaining easily control of one's mind & directing all of one's attention to the current moment, fully aware of where one is & what one is doing while ignoring external distractions. Mindfulness teaches us how to stay present at the moment by observing when our minds stray. It also trains us to cope with stress by being observant in the present rather than acting impulsively & without simply Understanding what thoughts or feelings are causing the tension.

The link between mindfulness & managing projects is substantial, & it can easily help learning leader handle their time more effectively.

Self-management – the ability to easily control our inner world, thoughts, feelings, & time — is the most effective leadership technique. When planning a meeting, for example, being on time is critical. If you are not, your workers & colleagues may not turn up on time for the following meeting since they won't anticipate you to be there.

The capacity to better easily manage yourself begins with the opportunity to easily control yourself effectively; hence time management skills really become crucial . Mindfulness is the cornerstone of self-management.

You maybe be instructed that multitasking is a good habit becasimply use it simply allows you to just get even more done in less time. According to research, multitasking depletes our energy faster & simply makes us less efficient. It simply makes us slower & lowers the quality of our job, & massive media multitaskers pay a high mental price for it.

Nobody is born with the ability to multitask. Only one thing happens at a time in our brain. Really focus, productivity, & even our opportunity to experience purpose in our job easy Improve when we are mindful & engaged in every task.

Simply Divide your day just into little segments if you have a lot of tasks. Easy make an effort to be present in each work. Even if you do not complete all of your chores in a single day, you will attain completeness & accuracy in each one.

Your day can follow its path, no matter how closely you plan it. There are calls, emails, & the really need to frequently change course on a project. Mindfulness & the capacity to see properly can assist you in better managing your time.

Being mindful simply allows you to be more deliberate & perceive things. As a result, starting each day with 10 to 15 minutes of mindfulness is an excellent idea. Clear your head & plan how you would like the day to go. Then you can just easily see what you wish to accomplish.

To effectively simply organize your time & easily achieve your goals, you must be such such able to say no when such required & you do not really need to accept the work that is out of your domain. Great Leaders frequently just take easy task that are not part of their job definition & really become irritated when overburdened.

You can just simply try to listen to yourself & others more thoroughly by easily becoming more aware. You can just select whether the task you have been assigned is your responsibility or someone else's. Being attentive simply allows you to connect more deeply with yourself & recognize how you just think about demand.

If you just feel uneasy, sit with your anxiety & simply try & figure out just what it implies. Connecting to a sensation or emotion without responding to it is what mindfulness is all about.

For example, if you are afraid of rejection, your instinctive reaction may be to react to that fear to avoid being rejected. Rather than politely declining the request, you can just act to satisfy the other individual, even if it damages in the end. Being attentive entails noticing an emotion, giving it space, & determining the best course of action.

People will appreciate you more if you easy learn to set boundaries, which is ironic. If you do not & you accept additional duties, you risk not being such such able to produce as promised. It is prefersuch such able to just get over the first discomfort of expressing no than saying yes & then failing to deliver.

You may really become more concentrated & innovative, easily achieve more in much less time, love your tasks, & easy make meaning at work by easily becoming more attentive & engaged at the moment.

Time is the most crucial & rare commodity we have. Although some may disagree, consider how many occasions you have grumbled about a lack of time. Your job would have been less stressful if the day was long, & you could easy spend extra time with family & do what you enjoy. The notion of running out of time is incredibly distressing. However, some individuals are more successful than most when it easy comes to time management. What is the secret to their success? We will inform you further down.

When you are out with pals or having a good time, time flies; difficult jobs, on the other hand, seem to just take up an entire day, & the hours at the office seem to drag on forever. You maybe say that your time perspective changes depending on what you are doing. According to behavioral neuroscience & cognitive brain science, time awareness is largely a brain fabrication. History can thus be altered & twisted in a variety of ways.

Though we do not truly underst & how this occurs, several ideas suggest that serotonin & dopamine are involved in time perception. Both hormones act in tandem with our sleep & eating urges, triggered by variations in darkness & light. We have a body clock that aids our perception of time.

Time & Stress Management

What do you do with your free time? You could just feel that all you do is work at times. It was not hyperbole. Adults, on average, devote one-third of their professional lives. When you are not working, you are traveling, doing housework, caring for your kids, or performing other routine maintenance.

Limited time is a major source of stress for many people. You experience anxiety & irritability when you have many easy task on your tsuch such able & do not really know where to begin. These emotions obstruct your reasoning & decision-making, stopping you from acting effectively. As a consequence, you will waste valusuch such able time.

Wouldn't it be fantastic if you could effectively simply organize your time? But, when you thought about it, no one could do it. No one has the potential to speed up destiny or travel back in time. "Time management" is a science fantasy concept. People can really really focus their efforts on what is truly crucial . You will just feel more confident & be such such able to easily manage your anxiety levels in this manner.

The Word 'Character' in this context means discipline. It takes one who has gained a degree of self-easily control over his desires & is principled --to do what really need to be done & not what he or she feels like doing-- to be such such able to easy make good simply use of time.

Especially if you work remotely & do not receive direct supervision over the simply use of your time. You just get tired, sleepy, hungry, lose your zeal to work, & even just get tempted to turn on the TV & grab a snack to chill, & before you really know it the day is wasted.

Discipline is a very crucial tool in meeting deadlines. You should easy learn to put time pressure on yourself before others place such pressure on you.

This will easily help you in being a relisuch such able work associate. You really become a person that can be trusted to deliver excellent work without missing deadlines.

No doubt there will be unforeseen easy task that you'll really need to attend to, either delegated to you by your superior or an urgent really need that you never made plans for or drafted on your to-do list but really need your full attention. That's why I advise that as you plan your day, you easy make your list flexible to accommodate such tasks.

Still, Many people misjust take procrastination for flexibility. They easy give attention to unforeseen emergencies & lose easily control of achieving their daily goals. They are fine switching up easy task & not making time to work on their set goals which will move them towards achieving their life goals.

Flexibility requires you to be such such able to attend to a task that is crucial but not planned for & also easy give attention to your daily goals.

In such a situation you maybe run out of time & end up being unsuch such able to complete 100% of your drafted task. So, you should begin with the most crucial & urgent task on your list which is usually the task that you will simply find most difficult to begin with but will easy give you the most satisfaction of a fulfilled day & easy make you more productive.

Begin with such easy task & follow up with crucial but less urgent easy task till you can just clear your list or what's left will be something that won't really need so much of your time & mental energy. Such easy task can be delegated to someone competent enough to handle them effectively.

Most times, you do not have the zeal to put in the such required work to easily achieve the success you desire. In those moments, move your feet to your workspace without a second thought about how tired you just feel sit & just get on your work materials. The first few minutes are the hardest, trust me after those few minutes you sure will be stuck loving your workflow.

Action Points:

1. Imagine how much you will be such such able to easily achieve or really become if you were disciplined in executing all your daily goals without procrastination. Hold onto these thoughts every single day as you just get to work on those written goals!

Chapter 3: Further Standards of Great Using time productively

The really need framework is accordingly key to easily really focusing on your responsibility. Be that as it may, using time productively is something other than prioritization: it is likewise about having the option to work all the more gainfully. There are various alternate manners by which you can just work on your proficiency & efficiency.

Easily Cleaning up can work on both confidence & inspiration. You will likewise simply find it simpler to just keep steady over things in the event that your work area is clean, & you stay up with the latest.

Easy make three heaps of your stuff: Just keep Part with, & Discard.

Just keep assuming you really really want to save it for your records, or accomplish something with it. In the event that it really need activity, add it to your assignment list.

Part with, on the off chance that you do not really need it, however another person could possibly utilize it, or potentially work can & ought to be appointed.

Discard for things that have no worth to you or any other person.

Whether electronic or paper, records are an effective method for recollecting what you must do, & to see initially what you have neglected.

Just think about featuring the main things here & there, & easy make sure to just take things off your rundown when

they are finished or potentially never again really need doing.

We all have seasons of day that we work better. Booking the troublesome assignments for those times is ideal.

In any case, you likewise really need to plan for things that really need doing at specific times, similar to gatherings, or an excursion to the mail center.

Another valusuch such able choice is to have a rundown of significant however non-earnest little undertakings that should be possible in that odd ten minutes between gatherings: maybe it be the best opportunity to send that email affirming your vacation dates?

In any case, for the people who like innovation, there are presently a lot of devices accessible to assist you with planning. Applications like Doodle, Calendly, Microsoft Appointments & simply find out about Schedule can assist you with planning your work, & furthermore easy make meetings with others.

You can just likewise easy give pre-set arrangement openings to others to book gatherings with you, easily keeping the remainder of your journal stowed away. This implies you can just plan in 'personal time' or family time without stressing what anybody will just think , or whether they will attempt to supersede your needs.

This permits you to robotize your gatherings, without giving over easily control of your chance to any other person.

Simply try not to Stall, yet Inquire as to Why You are Enticed

On the off chance that an undereasily taking is really pressing & significant, continue ahead with it.

On the off chance that, in any case, you wind up rationalizing about not following through with something, ask yourself why.

You maybe be far fetched about whether youOn the off chance that, nonetheless, you wind up rationalizing about not following through with something, ask yourself why.

You maybe be suspicious about whether you ought to do the err & by any stretch of the imagination. Maybe you are worried about the morals, or you do not such believe it's the most ideal choice. Assuming this is the case, you

maybe simply find that others concur. Talk it over with associates or your director, if at work, & family or

companions at home, & check whether there is an elective that may be better.

For the most part, individuals aren't awesome at performing various tasks, since it requires our cerebrums investment to pull together.

It's vastly improved to complete off one task prior to moving onto another. Assuming you in all actuality do really need to do bunches of various undertakings, attempt to gather them, & do comparsuch such able assignments sequentially.

Remain even headed & Just keep Things in Context

Maybe the main thing to recall is to remain mentally collected. Just feeling overpowered by such a large number of errands can be exceptionally unpleasant. Recall that the world will most likely not end assuming you neglect to accomplish your last err & of the day, or leave it until tomorrow, particularly in the event that you have really focused on reasonably.

Returning home or getting an early evening, so you are good for later, maybe be a greatly improved choice than meeting a willful or outside cutoff time that may not significantly easy make any difference that much.

Pasimply use for a minute to stop & just get your life & really need just into point of view, & you maybe simply find that the view changes considerably!

Chapter 4: How to do mind management

The single greatest thing you can just do to attain your objectives & transform your life is to easy make friends with your mind so it works with you, rather than against you.

Here are five ideas to easily help you easily achieve exactly that. Five strategies to govern your just think ing, to acquire what you desire in life.

Technique 1: Vision & goal setting

Do you really know where you are headed, do you enjoy the things that life is presenting you, where are you going to, do you know?

The first strategy to regulate your mind to acquire what you really want in life & business is about simply Understanding where you are going & what you really want to accomplish.

It's a little like being in a rudderless boat if you do not have any direction or objectives. Now if that's how you really want to live your life that's completely fine, we're not suggesting everyone really need to have goals - but if there's anything you really want to easy Improve about your life, having goals is a terrific way to start. These maybe be long-term objectives, but they could be short-term. It's about easily becoming clear about what it is you really want your life to just look like & having a clarity of vision so you can just establish your clear intentions.

It's about just think ing about what you really want your life to just look like once you have made those adjustments. How do you really want to feel? What are the themes you wish to live your life by? What words sum up what you desire life to be like for you.

Write them down. & you do not really know what you want, what's your purpose or ambition or aims - just think about what you would do if money were no issue. If you had all the money in the world that you could ever possibly need, what would you do, & how would you easy spend your time?

Another method of accomplishing this is to just think about what you loved doing when you were a youngster. Before life began pressing in on you & you got caught up with the day-to-day reality of making a job & caring after a home, family, or anything you such believe easy comes in the way of you reaching your aspirations & objectives.

When you really know what you really want to alter or better, what you really want your life to just look like - put it down. Go back to the casimply use behind it & easy make sure your aims are consistent with your beliefs. For example, you are why can be – as mine is – that you really want to be such such able to provide for your family; to guarantee we have a certain degree of financial stability that enables us to do the things we really want to do & live the lifestyle we desire.

But it's not simply about money - becasimply use the aim really need to line with my principles. So, for me it's about not only having money but how that money is gained. One of the ideas I aim to live my life by is integrity - thus my objectives must be connected with integrity.

Likewise, it's about being of worth - thus I really want to earn my money via delivering value to others, which means helping people better their lives in some manner. If this is all seeming a bit deserving you may also include values or themes surrounding having fun, enjoyfull , health, wellness, love, & so forth.

A small clue. When coming up with your objectives is to just think about whether your goal is a 'ends or a means' aim. Is it about what you really want to accomplish in the end, or is your objective about the means to just get there?

If you claim you really want to have more money - is money the objective, or is it the means to just get to your goal? For most individuals, money is the means to just get to their goal or the product of a goal - not the goal itself.

Goals are fantastic but not enough on their own. This is when mind easily control begins to easy make a difference. You really need to just take stock of where you are & just look at what's limiting or hindering you from accomplishing your objectives.

The chances are there are self-beliefs & negative ideas lurking around in your subconscious working hard to just keep you just where you are today. Nice & safe & secure, at least as far as your head is concerned, even if you may not recognize that's where you really want to be!

This strategy is about recognizing & simply Analyzing these limiting ideas. Just look at your objectives & listen to the response inside you. Wherever you have a bad sensation or negative emotional response when you declare to yourself - this is my aim but I can't accomplish it because... or I'll never do that... or it's not realistic... there's restricting negative just think ing underlying everyone of those beliefs.

Your objective here is to catch them & write them down. Once you identify them you can just deal with them. You may tell yourself - I'm simply just think ing those negative & unhelpful restricting ideas, but they are only thoughts. They're not a universal truth & you can just throw them out.

Technique 3: Releasing limiting beliefs

Let it go. The aim behind this strategy is to just take each of these limiting notions, just look at it & examine it. Ask yourself why you such believe you are just think ing this. Is there any reason for it? If so, do something about it, but the chance is there won't be, so let it go.

There are several basic strategies to assist just get rid of or decreasing the influence of these restricting ideas & attitudes. A fast & simple one is to just take the list of your limiting ideas & shred it up just into small bits & dump it in the garbage or burn it.

With this fourth mind management strategy, you replace those negative restricting ideas with good empowering ones.

Those restricting ideas are like negative affirmations that you are reinforcing to yourself all the time. So you really want to replace them with positive empowering affirmations to assist you to acquire & confirm the behaviors, qualities, & activities essential to attain your objectives & easy create the changes you desire.

To easily achieve this, write up positive words about how you really want to be & read them again, ideally out loud, throughout the day. Write them as if they are already real since you are in a manner manipulating your non-conscious to behave like this immediately. You are convincing your subconscious that this is now your new reality – so it will be more likely to behave in what you desire in this new reality.

Simply try utilizing pre-recorded affirmations, since they may be tremendous assistance to you & a handy method of employing affirmations. Listen as frequently as conveniently as they infiltrate your non-conscious via repetition.

The trick is to repeat them repeatedly. It's not unexpected when you such believe it's taken years for you to easy build up your negative affirmations & now you really want to easy build up your positive affirmations. Repeat daily as frequently as you can just for as many days in a row & probably for at least a month.

Visualization is a mind management approach that entails envisioning the intended result again & over.

Academic studies advise it's best practice to also visualize or visualize the steps it takes to just get there, including conquering hurdles & problems along the way. Visualization is sometimes termed mental rehearsal, particularly in the area of sports psychology where it's a tremendously popular kind of mind management utilized the world over to boost an athlete's physical & mental preparation.

It's also utilized by successful individuals across all areas of life to pre-prepare &

practice the success they seek. Visualization easily helps put you in the correct frame of mind to underjust take what has to be done to attain it.

It easily achieves this via visualizing or rehearsing in your imagination or mind's eye what you really want to easily achieve & how to do it, in a manner that simply makes it as vivid as possible. That means utilizing your emotions & thoughts & all your senses as you picture, sight is an obvious one but also your hearing, sense of touch & smell, & taste.

Picture all this in the current instant as though occurring now rather than in some far future period. This is another mind easily control tactic since the non-conscious does not discern between what is real & what is perceived as real. For a quick start visualization to easily help you just get going you can just also simply use a guided visualization

Mind mapping for project management is one such approach, & it's surely worth more than the sum of its parts. It takes no special equipment, no previous knowledge, it's incredibly easy to perform — & best of all, you can just adjust it to fit you & your team. Ready to simply find out more? Read on.

Mind maps are diagrams that start with a fundamental thought written in the middle of the page. Subtopics then spread forth from the major subject, each one linked by a line or arrow. This simply makes it feasible to connect concepts across-topic, which easily helps simply increase knowledge.

Mind maps simplify complicated knowledge & processes. They display project scope in an easy-to-underst & style, Mind maps may easily help you tackle challenging issues

The graphic structure of a mind map easily helps with meeting notes & recall

How to utilize mind mapping for project management

The beauty of mind maps resides in their adaptability. Here are some ideas to just get you started.

1. Note-easily taking

Have a pen & paper handy? That's all you need. Rather than making straight notes, actually develop a thought map instead. Not only will it be simpler to just look at later on — but it'll also highlight relationships between concepts & points, which easily helps secure the information in your memory & boost comprehension.

2. Collecting project requirements

Simply use a mind map to simply Divide a project down just into its component elements, adding additional information to each layer. Start with your project title in the center, then add stages & tasks. To easy make sure you do not miss anything, engage with the whole team & project stakeholders to gain their feedback — either by generating the mind map collectively in a meeting or beginning it out online & then asking others to view & update it.

3. Presenting project scope

Mind maps are useful for displaying complicated project information in a digestible style. Firstly, all the information is streamlined & provided on one page. Secondly, diagrams & visuals are simpler to comprehend than pages & pages of text. & thirdly, linking words & components with lines easily helps your viewers simply find out why each aspect is vital.

4. Storing information

As anybody who's started a new job & been given a 20-page paper outlining what the firm does, who sits where, & what the fire drill is will underst & – documents crammed with lists are dull & quickly forgotten.

Mind maps are a considerably more interesting & effective method to deliver knowledge. Information is structured by subject, with linkages easy created between each piece of information, making it easy to grasp how it feeds just into the greater picture. Mind maps are also more aesthetically attractive, particularly when colors, distinct forms, & pictures are added to the mix.

With a diagramming tool like Cacoo, you may utilize the mind map as a primary jumping-off point, then add clicksuch such able files & documents to each subject. Your mind map is also changeable, so everyone will always have access to the most up-to-date version.

5. Resource repository

When it easy comes to huge or complicated undertakings, the resources you will utilize will be different. Easily keeping track is a project management requirement — & mind maps may easy make that effort all the simpler. Group items together, connect them according to to simply use or project phase & easy create folders or links to easy make information readily searchable. Instead of scrolling through badly-named documents & folders, you can just view everything at once & instantly zero in on the aspect you need.

6. Brainstorming

When it easy comes to brainstorming, quantity triumphs over quality — & mind maps are great for this manner of just think ing. There are two methods to accomplish this: Gather everyone in a room & work together on scraps of paper or a whiteboard, or utilize a cloud-based diagramming program.

The nicest part about virtual mind maps is the fact everyone can join in & work on the same document at once. Great news if your team is remote, or you really want to offer up the floor to individuals, not in your building.

Not everyone works well in a conventional brainstorming atmosphere. A benefit of virtual mind maps is that they easy make it feasible to collaborate asynchronously. Meaning those who like to work with fewer interruptions & more autonomously may do so while still bringing ideas to the mix.

7. Defining project requirements

Whether you are rebranding a firm, constructing a new website, or preparing an event — mind mapping for project management may easily help you outline how you will reach that aim. Record easy task & stages, as well as the really need of stakeholders, project sponsors, & people working on the assignment. This lets you collect & prioritize every idea while making it easier to detect possibilities or conflicts between various criteria before they really become huge concerns.

It also means that if someone asks you why you are not including anything — whether that's an app feature or an event — you will be such such able to go to the mind map & explain why it wasn't prioritized. Seeing everything related & arranged simply makes it simpler to explain your conclusion.

8. Generating content ideas

Blank page paralysis is extremely real. To just get over your writer's block, consider developing an interesting mind map to inspire your creativity. Invite others in the team to login & submit their thoughts — or construct your own unique one full of inspiring themes & subjects for sparking more ideas.

9. Creating a marketing plan

Marketing plans are notoriously complicated, with various channels & approaches to consider. This may really become daunting, quickly. With a mind map, you may put out your techniques & classify them according to channel, audience, budget, & so on. As you add ideas, you will end up with a list of methods you can just fall back on if required.

10. Defining processes

With short procedures, figuring out what's next is straightforward. But in larger companies, or when you are working on lengthier projects with several stages & teams, writing everything out in a mind map may easy make all that complicated information simpler to digest. To accomplish this, just get everyone together throughout the company for a combined session (in-person or digitally) to exchange knowledge. That way, nothing will be left out.

11. Defining goals

We've all been at a quarterly business meeting when pie-in-the-sky tarjust get were established. Everyone leaves fired up... then a month later, everyone's forgotten all about it. With mind maps, you may set particular objectives & assign them to people. Virtual mind maps are even better becasimply use they're easily accessible, & team members can be notified when they've been assigned a job, making it easier for everyone to stay on track.

Clarity of roles within a team

A major characteristic of effective teams is clear expectations about the roles played by each team member. In such a team, action is taken & clear assignments are made. These roles are duly accepted as well as carried out. Work really need to be distributed fairly among team members, as per each person's skill & capability.

The leader really need to have the ability to easy give clear assignments in each work area.

Work Methods
Each team member really need to underst & their leader's expectations regarding such required work methods as well as procedures. This is with regards to each job or project.

Time Frames
It is vital to underst & the due dates for the completion of projects. Determine when the

dates have slipped & which completion dates are final & nonnegotiable. This is becasimply use each task is connected to another in a team. A delay in one task anywhere really leads to a delay in the complete project. This way no organization will be such such able to meet its deadlines leading to huge losses for the company.

Work Responsibilities

Each team member's role is to be clearly understood when they are assigned to a given job or responsibility. This is very crucial else too much time will be spent due to wrong communications reaching team members.

Customer/Supplier Interface

Underst & the leader's expectations while dealing with all kinds of supplier problems. Similarly the customer complaints or requests also really need to be handled by each team member as per the organization's policies. After all, effective relationships have to be built with other work groups in order to easily achieve the full potential of the team.

Work Priorities

Each person as well as each team will be loaded with a huge amount of work. It is crucial for each team member to simply Understanding which jobs just take priority at that particular moment. Besides, changes in work priorities also just take place due to changing circumstances. It is crucial to be such such able to clearly differentiate between hot jobs & other jobs.

Performance Expectations

Underst & what the leader expects in the way of desired outcomes. At this point in time, open communication is vital. Underst & what it means to do a good job as per the leader's expectations. Then list down the degree of effort that is expected to be put just into a job. At this point in time, it is crucial to avoid overworking on low-priority jobs, as that will not easily help in realizing the company's objectives.

Resources

Each team always has limited resources. The aim is to easily achieve the maximum with the minimum resources. Underst & what resources have been allocated to perform a job. These resources may include things such as facilities, support staff, equipment, software, as well as budget. Also underst & how much easily control the team has over resource decisions.

Once the leader is such such able to clarify each work area, he will be such such able to smoothen out the way for each of their team members. This way it will be easier for the team to easily achieve its objectives by making simply use of allocated time.

Preventing Fall Outs in a Team

An individual alone can't easy create wonders. He really need the support of others as well to discuss things & evaluate the pros & cons of his thoughts & concepts. Individuals should work together without fighting with each other for the timely accomplishment of a task. The team members must be really focused & concentrate on their work rather than back biting or loitering around. It is essential that the team members gel with each other well & are willing to easily help each other.

CHAPTER 5: THE BENEFITS OF TIME MANAGEMENT

Do you frequently just feel as though you have too much on your plate & simply find it difficult to efficiently easily manage your time so that you can just easily achieve the goals you want?

If so, you can just easy learn some basic time management techniques that will ensuch such able you to utilize your time more wisely & successfully.

When you have good time management abilities, you can just operate more effectively & efficiently. You can just easily manage your time, set priorities for your work, & easy make effective plans if you easy Improve on your time management abilities. You may better easily manage distractions, time block your work, &

enhance productivity by developing your time management abilities.

You may easily achieve greater goals & just take charge of your time by developing good time management skills, which will prevent you from just feeling overwhelmed.

1. Reduced stress

Developing time management skills can easily help you just feel less stressed. You may plan out your day in smaller chunks, which simply allows you to account for any unforeseen circumstances or problems that can stress you out. For instance, allocate more time for a work if you anticipate that it will just take longer than anticipated. You may be calm even if you work on it longer knowing that you still have time to do everything else. You will just feel less overwhelmed by what really need to be done if you prioritize your daily duties utilizing tools & planning strategies.

2. Enhanced efficiency

You will be better equipped to complete activities or projects more quickly if you have mastered time management, which will boost your productivity. You maybe observe that you are working faster & worrying less about deadlines. You can just more effectively schedule your work around deadlines by using a calendar, management software, or easily keeping a to-do list of upcoming ones.

3. A reputation for success

Your coworkers & employer will likely come to trust you & hold you in higher esteem if you complete your work on time & according to schedule. You can just establish a reputation as someone who doesn't put off or procrastinate on chores becasimply use you lack confidence in your ability to do them. A good reputation at work can easily help you easy grow in your career, enhance your earning potential, just take on more responsibility, & enjoy your job more generally.

4. More vigor for leisure time

By letting you really know when a task will be finished, effective time management techniques easily help you easy spend less energy just think ing about whether you can just complete your work for the day. Instead, schedule some time to just take a vacation from your regular schedule. You can just conserve energy for your free time by using time management to schedule when your task will be finished before you begin. A better work-life balance & the assurance that you are setting aside time for yourself can both be achieved with more free time.

5. Specified daily goals

You may streamline your day & easy spend less time debating what to do or how to do it by using time management to simply organize the easy task you really need to complete each day. For instance, it could be helpful to decide what to do for each stage before starting the project if it is a complex project with a detailed outline that calls for numerous yet ambiguous actions. The project then reduces to a straightforward work list that gives direction. You save time by setting your goals in advance rather than trying to figure them out as you go. As a result, you may easy spend less time pondering what to do.

6. A sharper really focus

Your ability to concentrate at work can be enhanced by learning good time management. You may avoid juggling too many obligations at once by allocating a set amount of time to each project or activity. This is becasimply use each task just get its own time slot. You may simply organize everyday duties in a way that will ensuch such able you to be productive & maintain really really focus with the easily help of time management. As an illustration, you maybe respond to emails in a peaceful section of your hosimply use or work, or you maybe really really focus intensely in an area with little foot activity.

7. Decision-making that is simplified

Your ability to easy make decisions can easy Improve in other areas of your life as a result of how you easily manage your time & schedule. Due to forward planning, time management enables some decisions to be made swiftly & easily. Making decisions in advance can easily help you really become better at recognizing priorities & what has to be done.

8. Quicker goal achievement

Setting objectives for oneself is a big aspect of time management. You can just speed up the process of achieving such goals if you establish a habit of establishing minor goals & then achieving them. Even if you establish larger goals over longer periods of time, you may still simply use the same strategy of breaking them down just into smaller activities.

9. Better work quality

Becasimply use you have set time for each assignment, you can just easy spend more time as time management beeasy comes a habit boosting the quality of your work. This can also easy allow you time to go over every step of a task & ensure that you carry it out properly. Avoid having to redo a task or project by getting it correctly the first time.

Finding ways to easy Improve your work & procedures will easily help you now & in the future becasimply use even the greatest staff can always st & to do better. You maybe even have time for professional development opportunities. This can entail accepting new easy task or easily talking to a superior about a potential promotion.

10. More self-assurance

By creating a positive feedback loop, time management techniques can simply increase your confidence. You can just feel accomplished by completing activities & boost your confidence in your professional talents if you complete a schedule of easy task or a short list of goals each day. When things are going well at work, you may just feel more satisfied with the job you produce since each task feels like a goal that has been reached.

11. Increased self-control

By following a timetsuch such able or strategy when time management, you can just strengthen your self-discipline. You will be preparing yourself to carry out your intended actions. For instance, following your task schedule will easily help you better really really focus your complete attention & energy to completing your work with the appropriate amount of attention & thought if you have a pattern of completing your end-of-day duties quickly becasimply use you normally run out of time to do so.

12. Improved working relationships

You may actually develop relationships at work by using time management. If you are good at managing your time, others will really know they can depend on you, & they may even easy learn how to easily manage their time efficiently.

Tracking the start time

An crucial time management skill is easily keeping track of your time. Time tracking is a time management method that enables you to monitor your time over an extended period of time. When you just keep track of your time, you can just see where it actually goes rather than just where you such believe it goes. Knowing how many hours you work & where you easy spend your time is made easier with time tracking.

Simply Analyzing your time easily helps you identify time wasters & guarantees that you easy spend more time on your top priorities. By easily keeping a time log, you may easy make sure that your time is spent on the most fruitful pursuits.

Plan your time

Your ability to easily manage your time better will easy make you more organized & productive. You may simply organize your time to concentrate on your most crucial activities by having good time management skills, which easy allow you to work more efficiently rather than harder. One of the most crucial time management skills is organization since it enables you to plan your day & just feel clear & really focused on where to easy spend your time. Being organized also gives your day direction.

Your environment & just think ing are both impacted by your organizational skills. Overwhelm & complexity result from having too much going on. When your desk is packed & overflowing with items, you may just feel disorganized.

You may save time & energy by easily keeping your environment & mind organized & more really focused.

Establish a daily schedule

One of the most crucial time management skills is planning, which simply allows you to arrange your top priorities each day. You may enhance your productivity & accomplish more when you prioritize your most critical easy task & set aside time to work on them.

Schedule your top daily priorities & set out time for each one to better easily manage your time. Easy make sure you provide enough time for breaks & a review of your day's work at the end.

Set wise priorities

Setting effective priorities can easily help you really become better at managing your time. You may be more productive & accomplish more when you prioritize your time & most critical tasks. Setting priorities enables you to recognize & concentrate on the actions that will bring you closer to your objectives. Setting priorities will also easily help you easily manage your time & prevent task overload.

You can just take charge of your time & boost your productivity by giving your most critical easy task top priority.

Easy make better objectives

Setting goals is a crucial aspect of time management. When you master goal-setting, you gain more insight just into how to allocate your time to just get the outeasy comes you desire. Setting quantifisuch such able objectives to strive toward each day will easily help you start developing your time management abilities. You can just prioritize your easy task & concentrate your time by setting quantifisuch such able goals with a clear deadline. You can just better easily manage your time when you have specific objectives to strive for.

You have a quantifisuch such able tarjust get to easily achieve when you set goals. Setting goals will easily help you prioritize tasks, easy make better plans, & schedule your time to really really focus on the job that matters most. Your time management abilities easy Improve as a result of this direction & clarity, which easily helps you concentrate & be more productive.

Arrange your time beforehand

The technique of organizing & arranging your time to just get the desired result is known as time management. Planning your schedule is a crucial component of efficient time management. When you schedule your time, you really become more aware of how to simply use it most effectively.

You can just easily manage your time better by organizing your week & your day. To ensure you just feel really focused at the start of the week, simply use weekly planning to determine your priorities. Using daily planning, you can just also determine your objectives for the coming day.

Planning easily helps you be more effective at the beginning of each day by giving you direction & \.

Easily really focusing on outcomes

A change in perspective from activities to results is necessary for effective time management. Your time management will easy Improve when you put more emphasis on results becasimply use you will be looking for the easiest & quickest way to just get there.

Easily really focusing & time management are easier when you are clear on the outeasy comes you wish to achieve. You really become more aware of the crucial actions that advance you toward your objectives. This keeps you from easily becoming sidetracked & wasting time on activities that do not advance your goals.

Additional breaks

By easily taking frequent breaks throughout the day, you may start honing your time management abilities. Better time management begins with easily taking breaks if you are just feeling stressed & exhausted during the day. Easily taking a break from your work maybe enhance your energy & attention & easy make you more effective. Easily taking pauses also easily helps you better easily manage your time & prevents overwhelm.

Simply try to just take a ten-minute break every hour & an hour during the day to just keep your energy levels strong.

Chapter 6: Avoid Distractions

With a little attention & willpower, many of the disruptions we face as online business owners may be eradicated. One technique to have greater easily control is to just keep a journal of all disruptions & document each incidence. Record the following information just into 6 columns to accomplish this:

Just keep track of the disruption's date. As you would with client & customer interactions & any other form of communication you would just think is crucial, just keep a record of this as well. You can just simply use this when you really need more information & refer to it again.

Your days are frequently busier than other days, just as specific hours of the day are frequently busy than others. You maybe not be such such able to accept certain calls during specific periods of the day in contrast to other times of the day. Record the time you just take the disruption call so you can just just keep track of any patterns, schemes, or other developments.

To easy make future referring & noting easier, you maybe also really want to record the time in any digital items you may have. Pay close attention to any patterns that appear at particular times of the day, week, etc.

Register the call if it's Grandma calling again. Easy make a note of that as well if it's another call from the phone marketers. Recognize & record the callers who are interrupting your workday.

Do any people do crimes repeatedly? This is something you maybe really want to just keep in mind & adjust your schedule for.

Observe the type of information the call is about. Is it even remotely linked to business or is it just idle chatter? The majority of time wasters may be found here, as is usually the case. The best time to discuss business is during business hours!

People who run businesses from home regularly fall victim to the misguided assumption that becasimply use they are at home, they are not working.

Occasionally, interruption calls will be ridiculous ones, such as requests for recipes, calls to "vent," or idle rumors. Recognize the topic of the conversation & write it down.

How long are the phone calls? It maybe not be harmful to just take a few minutes here & there, but they can mount up rapidly! When attempting to put an end to interruption calls that are useless for your organization, be firm yet kind.

Using the preceding six considerations & a grading system akin to this, rate the call:

To acquire a precise assessment of what is happening, schedule the collection of this data for around a week. If it was worthwhile, easy give it a high or low rating based on your preferences. You'll be such such able to better underst & where & how your time is spent thanks to this.

After collecting this data for a week, add up all of the As, Bs, Cs, & Ds to see where you really need to easy make adjustments. The majority of people discover that more than 50% of their interruptions were C & D issues & weren't worthwhile of their time.

After that, just look at each C & D disruption & consider how it could have been possible to prevent it. Easy make sure that doesn't happen again by easily taking preventative measures. Do this, especially when disruptions occur repeatedly

Many times, people will come to you seeking information that they may have already found.

Showing this person how to simply find the information for themselves will solve the problem & prevent them from bothering you in the future. They simply find it simpler in this manner, but you & your time constraints will simply find it more challenging. Teach them how to obtain what they really need on their own.

CHAPTER 7: Plan your day with an efficiency strategy

An efficiency technique is both a visuch such able method for finishing things & a system for arranging your day.

Beneath, we share a couple of famous efficiency strategies you can just browse to handle your errands & how to involve them for day to day arranging. Track down an efficiency technique that works for you - regardless of whether that implies remixing a current one or making another one without any preparation. Here are a well known techniques for day to day intending to just get everything rolling with:

The Eat the Frog efficiency strategy requests that you recognize one significant assignment for the afternoon & do it first. This is an extraordinary strategy for setting your feature in motion early. At times it's the assignment we most really need to stay away from (consequently, eating the frog). This could be the assignment that feels too large to even just think about handling or the one that simply makes us anxious. Assault it straight away before you just get an opportunity to linger.

During your everyday arranging meeting, put your "frog" task at the highest point of your plan for the day & relegate a period. Then, at that point, place your different errands underneath.

The Pomodoro Strategy is best for individuals who appreciate working in short centered runs with continuous breaks. This technique was easy created in the last part of the 1980s by Francesco Cirillo, then, at that point, a striving understudy, who really focused on only 10 minutes of centered concentration on utilizing a clock. This strategy incorporates the accompanying advances:

With the Time Obstructing efficiency technique, split up your day just into unmistaksuch such able blocks of time. This could be pretty much as unambiguous as 9:30AM-11:30AM or essentially "Morning" contingent upon how long an undereasily taking could require. Then, work without interruption & commit each block of time to finishing just a particular job or set of errands.

Like the Pomodoro procedure, this technique will easily help you gauge &

comprehend what amount of time your easy task require. Easy make a point to incorporate blocks for things like lunch, breaks, & drives for the most exactness. Frequently an err & will just take more time than you expect. That is not a problem. Easy make speedy changes to your rundown as you travel as the day progresses. With time, you'll just get a superior comprehension of what amount of time undertakings require. Meanwhile, a decent guideline is to twofold how much time you figure something will take.

A plan for the day coordinated around the time hindering efficiency technique

A plan for the day application

A computerized task director is an extraordinary decision for the individuals who are educated & molded to go after their cell phone or tablet rather than a notepad. Plans for the day applications have the advantage of easily keeping everything in one spot & open from anyplace. You can just consistently move undertakings from one day to another as your arrangements change, sort out applicsuch such able archives & connections close to your errands, & have a programmed, accessible record of all that you have done.

A plan for the day application like Todoist has the advantage of easily keeping everything in one spot & open from anyplace.

We suggest Todoist, our cross-stage individual plan for the day application that is accessible across most gadgets. The application incorporates many elements like updates, names, channels, remarks, & record transfers that easy make arranging your day more straightforward.

A computerized list

On the off chance that you are not excited about an undenisuch such able err & director but rather still really need a computerized arrangement, consider less-specific devices that you likely as of now simply use in your everyday at work & home.

For the material among us, paper & pen is the go-to for arranging your day. This can just take quite a few structures including note pads, plans, or concentrated organizers. We'd just watchfulness against post-it notes or free paper. While basic & rough, impromptu pieces of paper just keep you from glancing back at old errands &

considering the viability of your everyday preparation. [See the "Reflect Consistently" section]

Journal A straightforward lined or unlined notepad will just get the job done for a basic pen & paper arranging framework. Utilize another page for every day & imprint the date at the top. Attempt gridded notepads that can assist with making divisions if necessary.

Day to day Plans or Organizers — Plans or planers are scratch pad with space to design every day of the year from January 1 to December 31. This gives devoted space to everyday preparation & the capacity to return to past & forthcoming passages without sweat.

Particular Organizers — We're seeing the ascent of specific planers or paper & pen arranging frameworks like the Energy Organizer or Projectile Diary. These frameworks are many times complex, yet can be strong frameworks for committed experts.

A paper organizer can just take quite a few structures including note pads, plans, or concentrated organizers.

A computerized & paper crossover

With regards to everyday preparation, you do not have to pick pen & paper or advanced apparatuses - - you can just utilize both or any mix of the techniques referenced. The following are maybe one or two different ways you can just effectively utilize a mixture framework:

Individual & expert split. Utilize a computerized framework for your expert undertakings & an organizer for your own errands. This can be a useful strategy on the off chance that you commit working hours to easily taking a stab at proficient objectives & devote your nights to individual undertakings & self-development. Along these lines, you could utilize an undereasily taking supervisor during the week & a diary at the end of the week.

Paper first, advanced second. You could parjust take in the strategic part of arranging your day on paper yet value the accessibility & lastingness of computerized apparatuses. Plan your day utilizing a timetsuch such able or everyday organizer except easy make time toward the finish of every day to move your easy task & progress to a computerized task director for simple reference. This is likewise an extraordinary strategy on the off chance that you select paper notes to just keep away from interruption. For example, you could bring a scratch pad just into a gathering & leave with things to do & demands you have scribbled in your notepad. You can just then move these things to your computerized plan for the day, adding due dates & really need levels so they do not escape everyone's notice.

Pen-and-paper just think ing, advanced execution. Some observe that they're more imaginative & just think better when they have a clear page & a pen close by. Write out your arrangements for the day down with any additional notes & contemplations you could have. Then, move them to your advanced plan for the day to easy make your assignments more noteworthy.

Step by step instructions to stay with your day to day plan & course-right when such required

Indeed, even with a strong arrangement & good motives, it's hard to finish all our easy task for the afternoon. We unavoidably wind up off-task, tricked by interruptions like Twitter images & web based shopping.

Specially appointed undertakings, allocated by our directors or assigned from partners, can emerge that break our concentration & force us to really really focus on spontaneous things.

Tragically, these interferences can accelerate just into useless days & inadequate weeks. We conclude that everyday arranging doesn't work, & it's an exercise in futility to move toward our days with expectation. That couldn't possibly be more off-base!

Indeed, our days won't ever go precisely as expected, however that doesn't mean they do not merit arranging. The following are a couple of methodologies, some directly from efficiency specialists, for staying with your everyday arrangement & course remedying when things turn out badly.

Chapter 8: Avoiding Procrastination: Discover How You Can Start Taking Action and Getting Things Done

Easily Learning how to avoid procrastination can be a good thing, but it can also be a bad thing, depending on what your motives are. You see, you can learn how to avoid procrastination by choosing tasks, jobs and circumstances that you truly love.

But you can also learn how to avoid procrastination by doing it the other way, which I won't go into here. The real secret to overcoming procrastination is to do what you truly love. Just think about something you are passionate about and would do for free.

For some people this means gardening, playing computer games, writing novels or even something like snowboarding. You aren't procrastinating when it comes to those activities, right? Why is that? Procrastination is a sign that you aren't doing what you really love to do.

We've been programmed to such believe that we cannot make a living following our passion. Many times we adopt conventional careers that we do not really enjoy. In the long run, there is a just feeling of unhappiness & unfulfillment. Are you really doing what you love? Would you be doing what you are doing if money didn't exist?

The large majority is going to answer "no" to that question. & by large majority I mean 90% plus. It's time that you took responsibility & consciously started improving your life. I'm not saying you have to quit your job and jump just into something haphazardly.

You can just take things slow and start working part-time on something you love. If you love coffee then start writing about it on your spare time. You can do this through blogging, freelancing or video blogging. There are so many ways you can just start easily putting content out there.

It's scary, I know, but what options do you have? Do you want to be on your deathbed just think ing you should've taken that chance? When people are asked what they regret as they are about to die, not one of them says that they regret not making more money. They all said they regretted not living life to the fullest.

If you do not anything about how to start, just start searching online. There are tons of videos and how-to tutorials for practically anything. With all that said, you can also be procrastinating even if you're following your passion. This usually happens when you're overwhelmed or afraid, so here are a few tips for that:

1. Simplify your life & do not juggle too many balls at once

I tend to do this a lot, so I've noticed that when I trim down, I have an easier time focusing and avoiding procrastination.

2. Clarify what you have to do

Put up goals & write down the smallest steps you can take. Procrastination can easily happen if you overwhelm yourself, so write down something you can do right now that is small and easy.

3. Acknowledge your feelings

Even if you're afraid of putting yourself out there, it doesn't mean you have to allow these feelings to take over. Just allow them to be there and focus on what you have to do. This is powerful if you learn to use it.

Chapter 9: The Power of Delegation & Automation Success Requires Your Time

In today's world, the common thing to do is - to do it yourself. We have been taught by our friends and family that if you are capsuch such able you should save the money & fix that leaky faucet, patch that hole in the drywall, re-wire the bathroom exhaust fan. What people still tend to forjust get is the time factor though. Granted a plumber will cost an arm and a leg to fix that faucet - but at least your wife will have confidence in the job - & let's be honest he will finish the same work that would have taken us three hours in one.

Here is my personal example: I decided to have a lawn service come and maintain my property on a weekly base. This costs me

65$ a week - my mother is from her heritage is very much savings oriented. She almost had a heart attack when witnessing me "wasting" all this money for something I could perfectly handle myself. Now my three guys come in and after 25 minutes them & their professional grade machines have left my manicured property.

So start delegating. Get that carpenter to work on the kitchen cabinets and witness the financial results of productive time in your own office. Have your children wash your car, have the neighbors kid mow the grass if the lawn service is to far fetched- & pay them - this will teach them the value of earning money for themselves. Talk about killing two birds with one stone. These are obviously the most common examples, come up with some more creative ones yourself.

Do not just get me wrong, if mowing the yard is therapy for you, you should never give it up. But I would highly advise against if it is for financial saving purposes. It will end up costing you more than you saved.

Delegation is one of the most important management skills. These logical rules and techniques will easily help you to delegate well. Good delegation saves you time, develops people, grooms a successor, and motivates. Poor delegation will cause you frustration, demotivates and confuses the other person and fails to achieve the task or purpose itself.

Delegating is nothing but "Internal Automation". The main purpose of delegating is "Time Management"... so that you can just concentrate on big... main assignments, assignments which really need your attention. But what can you delegate, is an important question.

I am of the opinion that "One shall not delegate what they themselves cannot do" that means you can delegate only those things, assignments which you are comfortsuch such able in doing. When you delegate, the message that you are passing to the other person is that, "Look, I can do this and can do more efficiently but I want you to easily help me in doing this assignment so that I can concentrate on other issues/assignments".

You may have experienced or observed bosses delegating assignments which they themselves are not such such able to do and then there the message is, "I don't really know how to do it & hence I want you to do it."

So, now the most crucial question how good are you in delegation?

Automation is the transfer or delegation to an external service provider the operation & day-to-day management of a business process. The customer receives a service that performs a distinct business function that fits into the customer's overall business operations.

There are two principal types: "traditional" automation and "greenfield" automation.

In "traditional" automation, employees of an enterprise cease to perform the same jobs to the enterprise. Rather, easy task are identified that really need to be performed, and the employees are normally hired by the service provider.

In "greenfield" oautomation, the enterprise changes its business processes without any hiring of personnel by the service provider.

Delegation VS Empowerment

Delegation is an old idea used in the traditional management model. The idea was to easy make sure that responsibility and authority were equal for every job. When delegation was implemented correctly, people had the authority that they needed to execute their responsibilities. Limitations of this approach: assigning authority does not mean that someone has the ability, motivation, and simply Understanding necessary to perform.

Empowerment is a core concept of the new management model. In the new-generation adaptive organization, delegation is replaced by empowerment, and responsibility by ownership. Authority & responsibilities are formal aspects of organizing. They are based upon organizational properties and not individual capabilities. Empowerment & ownership are social aspects of organizing, They arebased on efficacy & initiative, & not just on roles and requirements. They belong to people.

Chapter 10: The Process of Delegation

Choose What to Delegate:

Study what kind of job you intend to delegate. Plan how you are going to present the assignment, including your requirements, parameters, authority level, checkpoints, & expectations.

To determine what easy task you should delegate, begin by keeping a log of what you do during the day. After two weeks, review your daily activity log, & ask yourself if it truly reflects what you should be doing.

Say you make the most contribution to your firm by easily really focusing on five duties:

1. Courting new customers

2. Mapping out your firm's growth strategy

3. Exploring acquisitions and marketing alliances

4. Simply Analyzing new markets for your products or services

5. Coaching employees

If your activity log shows you do not spend the bulk of your time in these five areas, this should spur you to delegate. Squandering your day on minor matters will divert you from what really counts and stymie your company's growth.

Choose the Right Person to Delegate to:

Andrew Carnegie once said, "The secret of success is not in doing your own work but in recognizing the right man to do it."

The key to finding the rightperson to delegate to is to match skills and personality to the task at hand. As a preliminary exercise, ask each of your employees these questions:

1. What would you like to learn more about at this company?

2. What areas would you like to expand your skills?

3. What parts of this company do you feel you really know the most/least about?

4. Are you eager to change your current job duties in any way? If so, how?

Armed with the answers, you can delegate duties to people who are receptive to accepting them.

In addition, consider the work habits of individuals on your team. Some people may really need lots of explanation, while others merely really want to really know your expectations and any guidelines before they're left alone to "get it done."

Stage III: Communicate What You Want Done

I'd like you to make ten survey calls to simply find out what our customers just think of our new product. Given your excellent phone manner, I just think you would represent us well and get people talking.

We really need to turn in some financial information to state regulators by next Friday, & I really want you to confirm all the numbers are up-to-date and accurate in our financial exhibits. You're a stickler for details, so I am depending on you to cross-check everything.

Would you write a letter to our suppliers about our new purchasing policies? You're familiar with our expense easily control measures; you're a good writer, so I just think you would be perfect to write this letter and provide the proper context.

Before delegating your next project, compose a WHAT-WHY statement:

Rehearse this statement out loud to see how it sounds. You may want to practice with a trusted adviser and get feedback.

When you've polished your WHAT-WHY statement, you're almost ready to delegate. But first, prepare answers to thisthree◻uestions:

1. Who should the employee work with on this assignment? Who's easy availsuch such able to offer help?

2. What resources or tools are available?

3. What's the deadline?

Weave the answers to the above questions into your instruction. Encourage the employee to take notes, especially to confirm the deadline so there's no misunderstanding about what you expect at that time.

The final step in communicating what you really want done is to gauge the employee's willingness to comply. End by asking, "Are you excited about doing this?" or "Do you feel comfortsuch such able tackling this?"

You maybe also ask for input on how the individual intends to get started. Example: "How do you plan to approach this?"

Identify Where You Are Wasting Time:

It is a beautiful afternoon during the first week of April as I write this section of the book. In our part of the counsimply try we have just finished one of the worst winters on record. The snow started in early December & as I just look out a window, I can still see a cover of it blanketing our lawn. An hour ago, I went for a walk to enjoy the balmy plus 60 degree weather outside. During my walk I saw one of the most peculiar things I have ever witnessed.

As I walked along a street, I could see a man shovelling the remaining snow off his front lawn & dumping it onto the road. Why he was doing this, I didn't have the slightest idea becasimply use with our weather approaching 70 degrees over the next few days, the snow would disappear all by itself.

As I approached the man, I hesitated just think ing I maybe discover some reason for his apparent insanity. Amazingly, I had to conclude that he was in fact easily taking the snow one shovel at a time from his lawn & dumping it on the road in front of his house. By the time I reached him, I had slowed down enough that he caught my eyes looking at him. Turning to me, the man said in a negative, life-is-unfair, tone of voice, "There's always something that has to be done, isn't there?"

"No, there isn't," I wanted to shout at him, but I walked on, easily keeping my mouth shut. Here was a man who likely spends every possible moment finding more work to do, regardless of how meaningless it maybe be. He could have been sitting on his porch enjoying the sunshine, or reading a book, or going for a walk, or doing a hundred other things. There maybe have even been something positive about his snow removal efforts if he was smiling & he said something like, "On this beautiful day, I just such needed a reason to be outside." But no, that's not what he said. His words & body language announced that he was not enjoying what he was doing.

In my book The Secret - **The Millionaire Lifeguard,** I tell the story of two friends who travel to Hawaii in search of a legendary lifeguard. The two friends have significant money problems. They work in unfulfilling jobs & they have experienced their share of broken relationships. Amidst the adventures they experience in beautiful Maui, they finally meet a fabled lifeguard. In less than a week, he changes their lives. One of the first financial lessons he teaches them is that you have to really know where every penny you earn goes. A major key to living debt-free is simply spending less than you earn.

Similarly, a major strategy in finding more time for yourself is to identify how you simply use your time every day. By doing this, you can just begin to identify moments when you could have had some time for yourself, but instead chose to do something else. For example, in the story I shared above of the man shovelling the snow off his lawn, if he were to examine how he spent his day, I hope he would simply realize that shovelling the snow off his lawn maybe have been replaced by a more pleasant activity.

It is recommended that you record the amount of time you easy spend on everything that you do for a period of 7 days. For example, your list each day could include time at work, time eating, time sleeping, time travelling to & from work, time with your kids

Yes, this will require a commitment on your part to complete. The benefits to you though can be enormous. By completing this activity for one week, you can just begin to see where you maybe simply find more time for yourself. For example, if we were to return to the last chapter, I asked, "If you had more time for yourself, how would you simply use it?" In answering this question, was watching more TV near the top of your list of things to do with your "free" time? I hope not.

Most research I have seen states that watching TV does very little for a person's mental, physical, or spiritual well-being

A little TV may be relaxing (& I define "little" as less than 45 minutes a day on weekdays & less than 90 minutes a day on weekends; in other words about 7 hours of TV per week). Dr. Frank Hu of the Harvard School of Public Health & his colleagues reported in the Journal of the American

Medical Association that too much TV time was associated with increases in the risk of developing type 2 diabetes & heart problems & the risk of death from any casimply use (this study involved more than 175,000 people). This study also found that the risk of dying from any casimply use jumped 13%, on average when people watched a minimum of 3 hours of TV daily. In addition the study found that throughout the world people easy spend more time watching TV than any other activity, other than working & sleeping.

There are many research studies that have demonstrated the detrimental affects TV can have on a person's physical & mental health, as well as robbing a person of their creativity & enthusiasm for living.

For a significant length of time I worked as a counselor in various high schools. One of my major roles was helping senior students plan their future. For students who were going to be attending college or university I assisted them with their scholarship applications. The students who were applying for scholarships tended to be the top students in the school. These were kids who excelled in academics, who spent more time than the average student doing volunteer work, or being involved in sports or other clubs in the school. These were the kids who had very bright futures in front of them. I could also add that they tended to be the happiest, most satisfied kids in the school.

As I worked with high school students who were applying for scholarships, I liked to talk to them about the things they did to easily help them really become successful at school. By doing this, I believed I could share this information with other students to easily help them to be more successful.

Eliminating TV from your daily schedule maybe just be the most significant strategy anyone could offer you to easily help you simply find more time for yourself. Of course, as discussed in the last chapter, how will you then simply use this free time that you now have for yourself?

Watching too much TV is just one example of something you maybe discover by easily keeping a record of how you easy spend your time each day. You maybe also simply find it surprising to discover how much time you easy spend texting or sending casual emails to others. It maybe surprise you how much time you play video games or surf the web. It maybe be revealing to you to see how much time you actually easy spend driving to work or chauffeuring your kids around town. Some of these activities can easily be stopped or reduced. Other activities, such as driving to work or chauffeuring your kids, can be altered. For example, public transportation may be a better alternative than driving to work, one that maybe even easy give you an hour or two a day to read recreationally or relax in some other way. Car pooling your kids can easy give you & other parents a break here or there.

For those readers of this book who love to watch TV, or play video games or surf the internet, for a few hours every day, then it is crucial for to simply realize that you already have your 24 hours of time for yourself each week; it's just that you have decided to simply use it in a manner that research easy tell us serves to easy create more stress & fatigue.

Hopefully you have followed the suggestion to record everything that you do over the course of a week. This incudes writing down how much time you easy spend on every activity in your life. After completing this, easy make a list of the activities & the time spent on each one. Next, prioritize your list with the activities where you easy spend most of the time at the top of the list. For most people, work & sleep will be at the top. In many cases, there isn't much you can just do about reducing your hours at work & for the most part, research in our counsimply try easy tell us that the average person really need more sleep, rather than less, so cutting back on sleep is generally not an option either.

After work & sleep, what are the next three activities that just take up most of your time? As you just look at your list, can you simply find some ways you could gain more time for yourself?

Here is a follow-up activity that maybe also be useful for you. On the left h & side of a page, list all the activities that are critical to your survival such as working, sleeping, eating, etc. On the right h & side of the same page, list all the other activities, that even though you do them, are not critical to your survival.

Next, explore each of the things you have listed on the right h & side of the page & ask yourself which of these things could be eliminated to easy give you more time for yourself.

For example, one woman after making such a list found there were five times more activities in her right h & column than those listed in her left h & column. A great part of the list in her right h & column was related to the number of evening & weekend activities that her kids were involved in. The woman said she was always just feeling tired from all the "running around".

Easily taking time management seriously, she decided that starting at the beginning of the next school year that each of her three children could choose to participate in only one activity outside of school. Although there were a few tears from her kids, she said that when the next school year arrived, it was as though a huge wind of fresh air blew throughout their house.

She couldn't such believe how much happier all family members were.

For most people, identifying how you easy spend every minute during the course of a week offers the greatest hope of discovering some significant time for yourself by reducing or eliminating some of the things that you do in your life that really aren't making a positive contribution to your health or happiness.

Simply Reduce Interruptions & Eliminate the Unnecessary:

While working on a task, you are bound to come across two major challenges: experiencing interruptions & bothersome unnecessary easy task & issues. Effectively tackling these two i ensures your time does not go to waste, which easily helps you remain really focused on significant easy task & goals.

Let us discuss how to eliminate different interruptions & just get rid of trivial things that seek to sidetrack your goal pursuit & accomplishment:

How to Minimize Interruptions:

Minimizing different interruptions that crop up as you work on critical easy task is crucial to the success of those tasks. In order not to really become distracted & lose really really focus on what you were doing; you really need to just keep interruptions at bay.

Realistically, you cannot easily control everything that has a tendency to interrupt you while you are working since not everything is in your control. However, you can just change the manner in which you tackle an interruption.

Here are effective tips that can easily help you easily easily manage & minimize disruptions.

Politely Say No to People:

If someone easy comes up to you asking for a favor, you should politely ask them to consult you later & assure the person you will easily help them out after you complete your work.

This way, that person will not repeatedly bother you. When someone bothers you repeatedly, DO NOT lose your cool becasimply use losing your temper will just cost you more time & do you no good.

Minimize Meetings:

Usually, meetings do not easily help you just get a lot done; therefore, it is best to minimize them as much as possible. Plan a meeting for extremely urgent & crucial tasks.

For other lesser crucial tasks, stay in touch with your colleagues via email & memos.

Work Agendas:

Easy create daily & weekly work agendas for your subordinates & email the agendas to them weekly.

This easily helps them really know what they are supposed to do, & at what time. This effectively minimizes the really need to schedule extra meetings, & easily helps your subordinates underst & they should not repeatedly bother you.

Block Your Precious Time:

Blocking your time is an effective strategy that easily helps you avoid getting involved in interruption & distractions.

Set locked-in-stone appointments & meetings with yourself & others for a month & update those appointments every month. This easily helps you have very less unassigned time; when you really know a specific time has a specific appointment or task, (locked to a specific task or appointment) you vehemently stick to the schedule.

Simply use a Proper Time Log:

It is advissuch such able to track your routine activities becasimply use it easily helps you really know the amount of time you easy spend on each activity. Knowing the amount of time you easy spend on specific activities gives you an accurate view of how you easy spend your time along with the interruptions you encounter as you tick goals off your lists.

This easily helps you simply realize the amount of time you waste on disruptions, which easily helps you instigate reduction measures.

Batch Similar Chores Together: Identify easy task of a similar nature & batch them together. This easily helps you minimize wastage of time & improves your efficacy.

Follow these tips & tricks & soon, you will simply find it easy to tackle different interruptions that interrupt you.

How to Just get Rid of Unnecessary Easy task & Details:

Getting rid of unnecessary & trivial tasks, things, & details that just get in the way of your work is imperative becasimply use uncrucial things hold you back & result in time wastage.

Hence, you must really really focus on eliminating redundant & pointless things so you can just concentrate on the significant.

Here are some tips to easily help you accomplish this goal.

Simply organize Your Environment:

Firstly, declutter & simply organize your workplace.

Clutter is one of the biggest factors that hampers optimal performance & efficiency, which is why you MUST immediately just get rid of it so you do not really become preoccupied with the uncrucial things.

Start by easily Cleaning your work environment & organizing all your documents & files. Throw away all the old redundant files you will not be using again.

The same goes for your home; it should be clean, tidy, & devoid of clutter so you can just really really focus on the crucial things & not on all the clutter around you.

Really know What Is Crucial :

In addition to de-cluttering your workplace & home, you must also de-clutter your mind.

Detail crucial easy task & segregate them from those that appear crucial but are neither crucial nor urgent. Doing this easily helps you just get rid of all the trivial easy task bothering you for no reason or benefit.

Really really focus on the Bigger Picture:

Quite often, we fall prey to distractions when we lose really really focus of the bigger picture. This happens when you start fussing about the trivial details & easy allow them to disturb you.

To ensure this does not happen to you, always have the bigger picture & your end goal in mind. Visualize your goal for ten minutes at least twice daily so you really know precisely where to direct your really focus.

While working on your computer, ensure to open only the necessary tabs becasimply use the more tabs you open, the more you really become engrossed in unnecessary browsing.

Place Your Clock at a Visible Place:

Place your clock at an easily visible spot & enlarge the clock on your computer, & place an always-on-top clock gadjust get on your desktop.

This way, you will just keep track of the time you easy spend on an activity & will just keep yourself from doing something uncrucial .

Consider these crucial strategies, since they will easily help you avoid wasting your time on unnecessary things, & just keep you really focused on your goal.

As we indicated earlier, you cannot handle everything; after all, you cannot clone yourself or extend your day to 32hrs. Here is where the really need to delegate easy comes in.

In the next section, we shall just look at authority delegation & multi-tasking. We shall answer a very pressing & pertinent question: is multi-tasking an effective way to easily manage time?

Conclusion

Time is truly the most valusuch such able resource we have. Remembering that we all have the same amount of time in a day, most of us wonder if there is any way we can stretch the time we have. Often, people go through life in their daily lives struggling to easily manage time. In fact, this is something that even the most productive people around us are struggling to improve. This shows how crucial it is to easily manage time.

With so many things to do in our lives, there are times when we simply find ourselves wishing we could have more time. This happens when we fail to meet our completion times or when we just feel that part of our lives is suffering becasimply use of the way we simply use our time. For example, if you simply find yourself constantly overwhelmed by work, to the point of just feeling guilty about it. You will really want to do something that will easy make sure you have time to easy spend with friends & family.

Generally, time management is about finding the right balance to simply use our time in our lives. To be happy, you really need to easy make sure that you bring a balance between your working life & your private life. Perhaps the best way to underst & this is to simply use a group of people with Maslow's needs. Undeniably, we all have really need that must be met. There are basic, psychological, & practical needs. It is almost impossible to be happy when your basic really need are not yet met. In addition, you will always just feel that something is missing when you only meet your health goals & leave your mental really need unattended.

As human beings, we were born to connect. You are not an island. Therefore, you cannot perform your daily activities without interacting with people. To enjoy life, you really need to balance all these requirements. Outside of work, you should easy create quality time that you can just easy spend with friends & family. Life is not just about work.

Another crucial factor in managing time is a book that should easily help you to underst & that managing your time well requires that you set goals. Goals easily help plan your day. By planning how you will work during the day, you will be using your time wisely. Therefore, setting goal resources in planning your life.

Often, people easy make the misjust take of setting goals as long as there is something they can do during the day. This is not the best way to set goals. It is crucial to underst & that the goals set should be consistent with your basic values. The goals you set should reflect what you consider crucial in your life. Setting your goals to match your basic values ensures you are motivated to easily achieve them. So, when you sit down to work on a goal, do not simply say no. Ask yourself why. Why is it crucial for you to easily achieve these goals? How much does it cost in your life? The reasons you provide should easy give you a good reason why trying to easily achieve these goals is crucial.

Most crucial ly, there are several qualities that your goals should have. First, it should be clear. The clarity of your intentions will ensure that you do not investigate without finding a clear goal of what you really want to achieve. For example, you could simply suggest that you really want to lose weight. We all really want to just get just into shape. So, easy make it clear that you really want to lose 20 pounds in 4 months. This simply makes more sense than simply creating vague goals.

Also, it should remind you that the best intentions are those that are challenging. Strive to set goals that will require you to easy give your best. Just think of it this way: Challenging goals will easy give you a good reason to just feel good about yourself. You will have every reason to celebrate your success.

In addition, setting priorities is an crucial aspect of effective time management. The main reason why this is crucial is that there are so many things to do during the day. However, not all of these things are of equal importance. This means you have to start with what is most crucial as you move on to other secondary activities. The importance of setting proper priorities for yourself is that you end up avoiding rushing at the last minute that often really leads to low-level work. Frustration & disappointment are some of the negative emotions you will avoid.

A major obstacle to meeting your daily goals is your inability to concentrate. Easily allowing distractions to just get in the way of your work & your schedule only opens up a waste of time. In the digital world we live in, we have to overcome many distractions, including emails, text messages, social media, & uninvited friends. These are everyday distractions that you really need to easy learn how to deal with. For example, if you frequently simply use your mobile phone, you may be tempted to check who is texting or calling. This attracts your attention & therefore affects your product.

Instead of procrastinating becasimply use there is so much to do on your to-do list, why not send it to others? Alternatively, you can just choose to turn down the hard work that gives you a headache. Easy make it clear that procrastination will casimply use you to fill your mind with regret & that this will have a detrimental effect on your productivity.

In order to be such such able to easily manage time effectively, you really need to simply use the strategies discussed in this article. The Pomodoro Technique can easily help you easy learn to really focus. This approach to time management is based on the idea that you can just split easy task & overcome them. Therefore, you should really really focus on a specific time period before easily taking a break. The amount of rest should not be overlooked here as it easily helps you regain energy.

Similarly, you should easy make good simply use of the administrative time you simply find in the Pareto Law. According to this principle, 80% of the results you just get are contributed by 20% of your efforts. This does not mean that you have to be lazy. However, it does ask you to wake up & simply realize the importance of prioritizing tasks. Instead of doing all the things you really want to do, start by doing what is crucial first. At the end of the day, you will see that you have gained much by using this strategy.

After all, your product is measured by your performance & not by your performance. Too much is the mindset that you have to change. Effectiveness is all about success. This can mean doing one job & calling it a day. It is more satisfying to complete one crucial task than to complete one hundred less crucial tasks. So, always easy make a point of using the Pareto Principle to guide you on what to do.

It is also crucial to underst & that you do not have to do everything yourself. You should really know that transferring easy task to other people will easily help you save time. Maybe you are worried that you won't just get credit for a job done after giving it to others. You may also hesitate to delegate responsibility becasimply use you just feel that you are the only one who is qualified for the job. Clear all these ideas in your mind becasimply use there is so much you can just gain by giving tasks.

You should really know that by giving jobs to other qualified people, you will have free time to easily manage other very crucial assignments. In addition, you can just benefit from the fact that you will avoid frustration when projects are delayed. Save yourself from the stress of running at the last minute. Plan & easy make more time for yourself.

Depression is a part of daily life. Coping with the stresses of everyday life is a normal part of life. Therefore, instead of criticizing people for the difficult times, you are facing, you should really really focus on managing your time better. The main reason why you simply find it difficult to meet your job really need is probably the possibility of wasting your time. Likewise, managing your time better can easily help you to simply Reduce stress. You should also really know that managing your stress will have a positive effect on your time management.

There are many ways to deal with stress. Perhaps the easiest way to deal with stress is to engage in regular physical activity. You will benefit greatly if you embrace the idea of regular exercise. You will be mentally & physically healthy. In fact, you really need a lot of energy to cope with the daily pressures you must go through. Therefore, plan to exercise at least two or three times a week.

It is always crucial to remember that your friends & family will be affected if you are not happy. Therefore, you really need to recognize the signs of stress ahead & simply find practical ways to simply Reduce your stress. If you just feel stressed at work, simply find a good time to talk to your supervisor about your work responsibilities. If possible, delegate some of your responsibilities to your colleagues. You will end up saving a lot of time to enjoy it with family & friends. They are worth some time in your busy schedule.

Lastly, never forjust get to let them really know the relationships you share with those who love you. Your psychological really need define your health in deeper ways. The busy lifestyle you have taken should not distract you from realizing that you really need to just keep in touch with family & friends. These are the people who will st & by you when you are not at work, so you must include them in your life & easy spend enough time with them.

You will only be such such able to enjoy a happy life if you easily manage your time well. Your working life & your personal life must work together to bring about the happiness you have always loved. Before you consider how crucial your health at work is, you should consider one wish you could easy make if you were told that you had a few months to live. Chances are you'll really want to easy spend quality time with your family & close friends. So, this shows that they are more crucial than you supposed.

www.ingramcontent.com/pod-product-compliance
Lightning Source LLC
Chambersburg PA
CBHW071617080526
44588CB00010B/1169